P9-CEO-912

For Arnie Levin – V.R.

SIMON & SCHUSTER
Rockefeller Center, 1230 Avenue of the Americas, New York, NY 10020

Copyright © 2004 by Charles Kreloff, Victoria Roberts, and Roundtable Press, Inc.

SIMON & SCHUSTER and colophon are registered trademarks of Simon & Schuster, Inc.

For information about special discounts for bulk purchases, please contact Simon & Schuster Special Sales: 1-800-456-6798 or business@simonandschuster.com

Designed by Charles Kreloff

Manufactured in Mexico

9   10   8

Library of Congress Cataloging-in-Publication Data is available.

ISBN 978-0-7432-6408-2

Is Your Cat Gay?

by Charles Kreloff and Patty Brown

Drawings by Victoria Roberts

A Roundtable Press Book

Simon & Schuster

New York   London   Toronto   Sydney

Have you ever found
yourself pondering your cat's
sexual preference?

If so, consider the following...

Do your shoes feel furry
in the morning?

Does kitty refuse anything
but filtered water served in a
martini glass?

Will only the finest
Egyptian cotton sheets do?

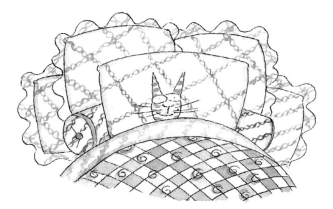

Does the litter box smell
suspiciously of Chanel No. 5?

Is kitty appalled by anything
less than sushi-quality tuna
served on Limoges?

Do you suspect kitty is using
your grooming products?

Around your house,
do hair balls take on a
whole new meaning?

Is this one of your cat's
usual stretches?

Does kitty's scratching post double as a shrine to Mother?

Does your cat insist
on traveling in a
custom-fitted carrier?

is the chaise longue his
personal catwalk?

Are your chairs
artfully distressed?

Does kitty transform
your mundane table settings
into something sublime?

Is your cat amused only by silk
spun by blind Belgian nuns?

Is kitty a bit too catty?

Do you come home and
find the lighting
dramatically altered?

Must every collar
have its place?

is the tom next door your
cat's "special friend"?

Is *Judy at Carnegie Hall*
always in the CD player?

Does kitty smoke just
for the effect?

Does your cat come in handy
as the extra man?

is everything
a musical comedy
reference?

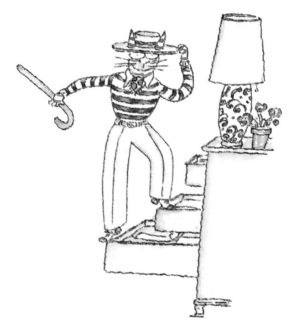

Do you suspect your wardrobe's been edited?

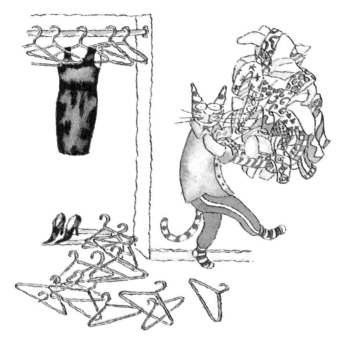

Can kitty sniff out a
knockoff at 20 paces?

Does your cat disappear
for hours on end?

Are kitty's the only paws
allowed near that special
collection of Barbies?

Has your first edition
of *Valley of the Dolls*
gone missing?

Do you have a
sneaking suspicion your cat
leads a more glamorous life
than you do?

If you answered these questions in the affirmative, then honey, you live with one FABULOUS cat.